The Simplest, Easiest, Fastest Step By Step Internet Marketers Quick-Start Guide To Making Money Online

Get Started Making Money With Your Online Business In A Snap

FREE
$357 of Free
Money Making Tips,
Tricks and Secrets
InternetMarketersGuidebook.com

By Michael Brooks & Eric Louviere

Cover by Jeffery Garza

ISBN #978-0-9857434-0-6

Published by Michael Brooks
710 Main St South, Box 1251
Southbury, CT 06488

www.internetmarketersguidebook.com

Table of Contents

About This Book

I met Eric Louviere in 2007. He was relatively new to the market and I hadn't actually heard of him when another marketer promoted for his coaching program.

I really liked what Eric had to say. And as I researched him more and more, I felt he was the perfect coach for me.

I was about to give up on Internet Marketing at that point. I was frustrated and had spent an absolute ton of money online without making a single dime. I decided to take one more chance and hire him as a coach.

The first thing he did was to teach me the very process that I will lay out for you in this book. This is the process he has always followed and he teaches to all his coaching clients.

Fast forward 5 years now and I am his business partner. We have several businesses we have launched together both offline and online.

Today, I teach the same strategy for creating an internet business to my coaching clients that Eric taught me. Once I began coaching clients of my own, I decided to put the process down in writing. What you will read in this book is the fruit of that labor.

Introduction

Welcome to this program. Glad to have you here. My name is Mike Brooks and I'm a full time Internet Marketer. I make my living working from home. And by the time you're done reading this, my hope is that you will be on the same path.

There's nothing better than this business. Here's why:

- I get to help other people
- I get to work in my pajamas if I want to
- When it's nice, I can work outside on my back deck
- When it's not nice I can catch a plane off to where it is nice and work from there
- I can work wherever in the world I want
- I can work whenever I want
- I have a ton of fun
- I get to help other people (yes, I said that twice.)

The goal of this book is to create a clear, concise and easy to follow launching pad that you can read in a few hours and get started fast. This is really what people want, to get started fast.

So this is a cheat sheet of sorts to do just that. Get you moving fast.

Why You Should Listen To Me

Because I said so, dag-nabit! Ok, I'm kidding. But listen, I've been there and done that. I make a full time living doing this.

I have VIP clients who pay me $3,000 to teach them just a portion of the same thing that's in this book. They gladly fork over that money because they know this stuff works.

Here's just one testimonial from one of my coaching clients.

"As someone who has bought a lot of info marketing products (perhaps far too many), I was excited to have my first coaching session with Mike, but my expectations where not sky-high. After all, I've read countless books, taken courses, and studied other marketers during the past couple years, was Mike going to tell me anything I hadn't heard or seen before? I thought I was just going to get some expert feedback on my ideas, which I was still thrilled about nonetheless.

*I was **blown away** during our session. Mike shared some concepts I had never heard before and **changed the way I look at marketing** and product creation. Changed the way I look at the marketplace and other marketers. **It was the best training I've ever had** –and it was just the first session!*

Mike is easy to talk to and extremely knowledgeable. He's very positive yet realistic and honest. His advice is practical and applicable. I feel lucky to have Mike as my business coach."

- Tom Litchfield

If you need more proof, just go over to my website mikebrooksonline.com or Google me. Together with my partner Eric Louviere we've generated millions online. We're pretty confident we can help you as well.

How To Use This Book

This book is a no fluff, no extra stuff, fat free, step by step manual. Pick the step you want to start with and do what that step tells you to do. That's it.

I can be a little long winded. I like to talk. But I've purposely kept all that extraneous noise out of this one. I want this to be so simple your cat can do it.

The important thing to remember however, don't skip a step you've not completed. Each is just as important as the other.

Most folks in internet marketing seem to be enamored with one thing and one thing only; traffic. So they jump to the traffic section. And here's how it goes:

- They skip all the steps and jump to traffic
- They spend money on traffic
- The traffic doesn't convert
- They get mad
- They blame me
- I tell them I told yah so
- I laugh at them for not listening

So the answer is to do all the steps. Even if you think you've already done a step, use it as an easy metric tool to hold your step accountable with. Read through the step and compare it to what you've done. If something is missing, fix it.

Don't get laughed at by me for not following the steps. Go follow them all!

Happy internet marketing!!!

Step #1 - Pick A Red Hot On Fire Niche

A niche is the business category you will operate in. Internet Marketing is a niche. It is also a sub niche of a bigger niche; the biz-opp or business opportunity niche.

Health and Fitness is also a very big niche. Within that niche you have sub niches such as diet, exercise, etc. Within diet there are sub niches such as men's diet, women's diet, diabetic diet, etc. The more targeted you are with your niche, the better.

If you've got a niche already, answer the following questions before you move on:

- Is this niche one YOU want to learn about?
- Does your niche have a ton of interest?
- Does it have a lot of competition?
- Are there a lot of people (buyers) in this niche?
- Is there a veracious appetite for information?
- Are people charging money for products?
- Are people charging a lot of money for products?

If your answer to any of the above are no, I suggest you find a new niche.

The above criteria are the only things that are important. Starting with, do you have an interest in learning about it?

Don't go and pick a niche simply because you think it's going to make you big bucks because you're going to end up hating your job. You have to find something that interests you. Something you want to learn about.

People often think they should find a niche with low competition. They incorrectly think low competition means they get all or a bigger share of the pie.

The fact is, if there is no competition, there probably is no pie. Besides, wouldn't you rather have a smaller piece of a bigger pie than the entirety of a teeny tiny pie? The correct answer to that is 'Yes'. Trust me.

When searching for your niche all that matters is the above. Your job now is to go find a niche that meets those criteria.

Market Research

To find your niche, the place to start is with research. You want to use the above criteria as your measure. Make sure whatever you choose is a yes when you ask those questions. Here's an easy checklist to start your research:

1. **Google keyword tool** – find keywords that have a ton of traffic with a ton of competition. Dig deep and get keyword ideas. The keyword tool is what advertisers use. Simply Google this: "Free keyword tool" and it should come up number 1. You will enter in your main topic and it will return useful keyword ideas based on the topic. Sort it by competition and you will see a lot of great ideas.

2. **Google your prospective niche keywords** in the general search. Once you do step one and have narrowed down some ideas, search for them. See what comes back in the results.

3. **Analyze the results** – are there products being sold, questions being asked, answers being give and paid traffic sending people to offers?

4. **Find the burning questions this niche has** by finding places where people in this niche hangout. What you want to know are the top 5 to 10 questions that almost every single person in your niche seem to ask. This is VERY important. This will tell you what your marketing should say and what your products should do. Some examples are:

a.   Forums
b.   Yahoo answers
c.   Linkedin Groups
d.   Facebook pages/groups of experts in your niche

5. **Review products offered by your competitors** through Clickbank which is a repository of online products, affiliates (also known as your competition. But in this case they offer a way for you to sell their product and make an affiliate commission.), Amazon, Ebay and any other places you can find where products are sold to your niche.

When your researching your niche, the goal is to find a huge, competitive and lucrative market. Then, to carve out a piece in that niche that is specific.

For instance, in the internet marketing world a popular sub niche is traffic. But you can break traffic down into even smaller sub niches. Like Youtube traffic.

That is part of a red hot niche but it is also pretty specific. Its laser targeted.

Copywriting Research

If I get into a room of marketers and ask them who is terrible at copywriting, most of the room will raise their hands. Why? Because it's fricken hard!

It's an art and a science. And to get really good at it means you have to commit to getting really good at it. And most people won't do that.

But a good copywriter knows the most important thing they need to sell is to understand what your market wants. So copywriting really starts here in market research.

This segues us nicely into the next step which is creating our squeeze page. As you are learning all about your niche, you should be taking notes to find the big itches. What are those burning questions your niche has about things (Step #4 from above)?

If you can scratch their itch, you'll make sales. So your goal once you find the niche is to uncover the burning questions they have. To do that means toiling in the forums and other places where real people may be asking real questions.

A shortcut is to find some trusted marketing. Find sales material from a marketer that you know is selling well. If it isn't a high converting offer, don't pay attention to it.

Review that copy with a fine tooth comb. Because they are practically telling you what your copy should be saying too.

They've done all the research and testing. Their product is selling and converting well. So all you need to do is uncover the problems and issues they are solving and then create your way of saying it.

Step #2 - Create A Squeeze Page

If you've got a squeeze page already, congratulations first of all because you're in the minority. Most marketers don't have one. Even if they've been in internet marketing for years.

This might just be one of the most important tools you will have in your tool chest. If you don't think you need one, guess again. You do.

I could go on for pages on why you need a squeeze page but I did promise I would keep this book short and to the point. So I will give you the main and most important reason I know of:

I do not know any internet marketers who make a full time living at it who do not build their own list. All the six and seven figure internet marketers I know all have subscriber lists. And to do that, you need a squeeze page.

If you already have a squeeze page, answer the following questions before you move on:

- Is it based on the marketing or on the product?

- Does it focus on conversions?
- Does it contain all the important elements of a squeeze page?
- Is it visually appealing?
- Does it have a sales funnel?

No, Do NOT Create The Product First!!!

I know what you're thinking. Why would I create a squeeze page if I don't have a product yet? Trust me, Grasshopper. I know of what I speak.

In the previous section on finding your niche, I told you to uncover the problems and questions people in your niche have. If you can answer the burning questions, you'll make money. If you don't, you won't. It's that simple.

What you want to know is those top 5 to 10 questions about what it is your doing that it seems almost everyone you encounter would ask you. If you were in a room of 1,000 people who you feel are your perfect prospect, what do you think they would all ask?

Find this and you've found the secrets to a vast fortune. This is what they want. This is what they will spend money on.

Now you can craft your marketing around this. Turn those questions into powerful, benefit driven bullet points with the sexy and the sizzle.

Here's some examples:

Burning question: How do I get free traffic to my website?

Bullet point with the sexy and the sizzle: How to drive red hot server melting traffic to your offer for FREE!

Get the idea? Your turn. This is where the rubber meets the road.

Your assignment is to uncover as many questions that your niche is asking. If you put every person in your niche in a room, what would be the five to ten questions they would all ask? This will be what you use to craft your squeeze page with.

The Marketing Will Create The Perfect Product

Once you have your squeeze page, you now know exactly what your product has to do. Now you have the blueprint you will use to construct the perfect product.

Just like building a house, you have the Architect design the plans. Then the builder just builds from those plans.

Your marketing should now provide the exact benefits your prospect wants. It should speak to them on an emotional level.

When you make your product do what your marketing says it does, you are now creating something very special. And you will be a hero to your buyers. And they will reward you by buying more and referring others.

Too many people design a product. Then they go back and create the marketing later. Many have to embellish in their marketing to make the sale. With this method, you will never embellish because your product will do exactly what the marketing says it does. And you will run your business with integrity and provide tremendous value.

The Important Elements Of A Squeeze Page

- Headline
- Bullet points
- Video (optional)
- Call to action
- Custom graphical header (optional)
- Footer with:
  o Terms of service
  o Privacy policy
  o Contact us
- Picture of you

The squeeze page below is a project I am currently working on with my partner Eric Louviere. You can see the page live at x2formula.com.

This is a classic squeeze page. The only thing missing is a graphical header. Eric has a strong name in the internet marketing niche so we decided to focus on him more than the graphic.

In the example below of Eric's Disclosure Journal, he used a graphical header.

The key requirements are present on both. Strong headline, bullet points, a call to action, which you see in the Disclosure Journal is above the-opt in box and in the X2Formula page it is below the bullets with an arrow pointing toward the-opt in box.

Each page has a footer with terms, privacy policy and contact us form. The X2Formula replaces the bullet points with the video.

Both of these squeeze pages, and most that you will see that convert well, have all of these elements. The page is very simple when you look at it. Headline, some body copy and a place to enter the email address. But the formula is powerful and works well when all elements are presented properly.

What Really Matters

The magic comes with the language used. At the end of the day, all the bells, whistles and pretty graphics don't matter worth a lick if you don't have the ability to effectively communicate your offer.

Enter the copywriter. This is not a corner to be cut. Copywriting is the most essential and important part of the process.

If you did your research from step 1, the copywriting should be fairly simple. However, the way you word things is very important.

The best way to understand good copy is to study good copy. During your research you likely found many squeeze pages in your niche. Study these. Learn the commonalities. Discover the rhythmic meter and power words used.

If you are not comfortable writing your own copy, hiring someone who is good at it can be money well spent. In our VIP coaching program, we review and critique our clients copy so that it is as good as it can possibly get. Each go through a rigorous process of writing and re-writing until it's perfect.

The best investment you can make is to find someone to help you here. At the very least, find other people to proof read it as a prospective buyer in your niche. If they are not compelled by it, you need to re-write.

Each niche is different, but in every niche there are a few certainties that you must try and work into your copy.

1: Persuasion – People are inundated with requests for their time and money all the time. There are many other things out there vying for our attention. You have to be persuasive to convince people to take action now. There are some fantastic books you can read on persuasion such as Robert B. Cialdini's book "Influence".

2: Power Words – These are more colorful and visual words. They take the mundane and boring and breathe life into them. Think of words that might add a bang to your copy and create a diary of them that you can pull from in a pinch.

You can say this: "Find prospects who want to buy"

But this sounds much better: "Laser target hungry prospects ready to buy now"

3: Button pushers – every niche has certain words that arose a sense of curiosity and desire in the prospect. In the internet marketing niche two words that work are 'fast' and 'easy'. Almost everyone in this niche wants to know how to make money FAST and EASY. Find these words and push those buttons.

4: Reason Why – Give the prospect a strong reason why you're giving them this free report. Or why you think they should buy from you. Or why they should do anything you want them to for that matter.

5: Urgency – People often times need to be given a strong urging to take action immediately. They need to take action fast before this offer is gone. Letting them know this offer could come down at any time or the price is going to increase.

6: Scarcity – This is only available for the first 100 people. Limited edition.

7: Benefits not Features – a feature is what your product does. A benefit is what your product does for the customer. A feature is an instructional exercise routine. A benefit is a simple fat melting program that gets you ripped fast. Everything should be benefit driven.

8: Don't Lie – There are a lot of marketers out there who promise things that are just flat out B.S. (that does NOT stand for Best Stuff). When you make a promise be sure that your product delivers. Not only is it just plain good business to do this, it's the law. Internet marketers have a lot of requirements based on regulations imposed. And more are coming down the pike for our industry. Understand these and follow them.

Step #3 - Rapid Product Creation

Unless you have a product you've already created before getting your hands on this little manual, or unless you have purchased a PLR or other type of pre-done for you product, don't start here first. I beg of you.

If you've gone and skipped ahead to this part, do me a favor and go back to step 1 and at least read a little bit. Most people make the huge mistake of beginning with the product first.

Those who do this are now in the unenviable position of having to convince the market to like what they do. They built it and are now waiting for the people to come. But when they get there, they see what YOU want them to see. Not necessarily what THEY want to see. See the difference? People want what they want. Not what you say they should want. Only Steve Jobs has ever been able to pull that off.

When you begin with step 1, you are learning what your prospect wants and desires. You are learning what it is that keeps them up at night. When you learn the solutions to their problems, you're going to create what they desire.

These steps are paved with gold. Imagine walking into a room filled with your perfect prospect and asking them what their biggest problem is. They all say the same exact thing. And then you build your product to answer that one burning problem. Do you think they'd be interested in buying that? Darn tootin' right they would be!

This is really counter intuitive to a lot of people because you are saying things about a product that doesn't yet exist. But now your marketing is the blueprint that you will use to build the perfect product.

Follow the Blueprint

The best part of following this process is you have now drawn simple plans that you can follow to build exactly what they want and what was promised. Many marketers who start with their product first find it harder to write copy. Because now they need to embellish and even lie to make the marketing look good and work.

If you're already an expert in this niche on this topic, you can get started and probably rip right through. But for many, you may not know the first thing about the topic. You may be helping a local business with this process in which case they're the ones with the expertise. Or maybe you enjoy this niche and just want to be in it but are not an expert.

But if you did the steps, you actually now have a great collection of knowledge on this topic. Now you just need to go back and find the answers.

Here are some methods you can use to create your content:

The Content Curation Method

One easy method to use here is content curation. This is finding content already out there and turning it into your own (without stealing).

When my partner Eric Louviere was first getting started, he went to EzineArticles.com and found several articles on his topic. He took those articles and put them into one document. Of course, he cited all the original authors giving them credit. Never steal.

This now was a brand new ebook simply using other people's content. And it sold well.

You may be thinking that no one is going to buy something they can easily find on their own. That's not correct. People buy things all the time they can get on their own. I pay someone to mow my lawn every week when I could easily just spend an hour of my time doing it for free.

If they want that information, they need to go search for it. You've done that work for them, thus justifying the value.

Become An Instant Expert

A big stumbling block for people is that they feel that they can't do this because they are not an expert. Everyone starts somewhere. No one is born an expert.

Here's the exercise to become an instant expert in your niche. And this is the exact exercise both me and Eric make our coaching clients do. Because this is the one that will really make you an overnight expert on your topic.

Spend 4 hours researching and taking notes on your topic. You can start on Ezine Articles but you can also go to the library and grab a few books. You can even buy 3 to 5 products in your niche.

Read through these and take notes. You must put in a minimum of 4 hours. It doesn't have to be all at once. You can break it up as you need to.

By the time the client comes back to us, they will know more about their niche than they ever thought possible. And their notes will provide the outline and content they need to create their product.

The PLR Method

Another method is to purchase PLR (private label rights) product. There are PLR product for almost every profitable niche. Just do a Google search on "PLR" and your niche.

Find a product or products and use this as a starting point. Find products that you have the rights to take ownership of and change. Then re-write it in your own voice. Add to it. Adjust it so that when you're done it is a completely new piece of work.

It is really important that you create your own product here. The PLR should only be used as a starting point.

You can re-write the entire thing. You can add to it. You can even use it as one component of your product.

Whatever you do, make sure you make it your own. Even though you have purchased the rights to put your name on it, just doing that would be a lazy marketer's method. Don't be a lazy marketer.

The Show Me Method

This is a method that I love to use. It's quick, easy and you can create powerful content off this.

In a nutshell, you're going to create step by step instructions. Show me exactly how to do a task.

To do this effectively, you need to chunk it down. When you look at a product as a whole, it may seem like it has a lot of moving parts. It looks complex on the surface.

This may make it seem daunting. Where do I even start? This is a huge reason many people start and never finish. They get overwhelmed.

How do you eat an elephant? One bite at a time. When you can make things extremely simple, then it's easy and fun to do. This is how to get things done.

So the most important part of this system is to break things down as much as possible. When you get to the point where you cannot break it down any further, it's time to create the content.

Here's the Show Me Method steps:

Step 1 – Section It

Break out your content into logical sections. If you're content is on how to drive traffic, your sections might be:

- Video
- SEO
- Articles
- Etc

Step 2 – Section Your Sections

Now take each section and break them down further. For example, how can you break video down? These sections might be:

- Video creation
- Syndicating
- Optimizing

Step 3 – How Low Can You Go

Continue breaking out your sections until you can't go any further. You could break the above down even further. Video creation could be chunked down into:

- How to film the video
- Equipment to use
- Editing
- Adding effects
- Etc

The idea is to keep repeating this process until you can't go any further. Your last list will be the instructions for doing the task. Now you can go back to the lowest chunks and fill in the blanks.

For example, the task of adding effects to the video may look like this:

- Add transitions
- Add bottom thirds
- Fade in the beginning and end

- Etc

Now you explain how to fade in the beginning and end. How to add a bottom third. Together these instructions fit under the section of adding effects.

You may then add a few paragraphs explaining why you would want to add effects. What it will do for the video and their overall marketing. How it relates to the big picture. Why should video creation be a part of your overall traffic strategy.

I like to chunk it out completely and then work upwards. But it doesn't have to be that linear. Sometimes as I am working on the details I get a clearer vision of how the big picture of a higher level works and I move back up and write.

However you work best is how you should work best. But using this method, literally breaking things down to the ridiculous, makes it so much easier to create.

To get my mind straight on how things should flow, I use bubbl.us. It's a free flowcharting tool. It helps me to see it visually. But you can also do this in a spreadsheet, bulleted list, index cards, etc. However you can best visualize and stimulate your imagination is what you should do.

Here is the sample I created in Bubbl.us to create this example:

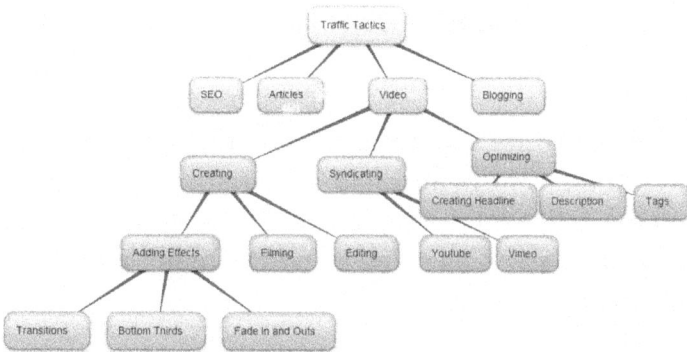

The Interview Method

When I first started in the internet marketing niche, I reached out to other experts to help me create my free product. I found someone who already had the expertise I wanted and already had the credibility in the market and asked if I could interview them.

By the time I was done doing the interviews-I did a total of 11 in all-I had a deep understanding and expertise on the topic. And now what I had in my possession was something that many people wanted.

You will find that many people who are actively making money online or leaders in their niche will want to do interviews. If they're selling products, they will want to get the word out about themselves and build their own brand. Being interviewed is a great way to do that.

Once you have interviews, you can deliver them as audios or get them transcribed and turned into PDF's. There are many opportunities on how to use this kind of content.

Conclusion

There are many ways to create your product. As you move into the next steps, you're going to find that you will come back here to create the higher level products as well. But like anything, once you go through this process, the next steps become much easier.

Your Assignment

The next step is the sales funnel. In that step, you will need to create multiple items that you can sell, in addition to your free give away offer.

If you know exactly what you're going to sell already, you can skip this. But most people get to this point and find it hard enough to pick a free offer to give. Coming up with more things to sell becomes even harder.

This exercise will help with this. Go back and do the Content Curation method. Take the time to take really good notes and learn a lot.

Then pick 5 things that you can give them for free or sell them. Later you will be able to go back through this and find what you will be selling them.

Step #4 – The Sales Funnel

At this point in the process, you're actually ready to start list building. And, you've done what about 80% of the market (if not more) hasn't done. Plus, everything from here on out will get a lot easier.

When myself and my partner Eric Louviere coach people, we do a lot of critiquing. The one thing we critique more than anything else by far is the squeeze page. Do you know why that is? Because most people never get past that point.

If you've taken action on every step, you've got a red hot niche, squeeze page, and marketing that is dialed in and ready to convert. If you wanted to get moving fast and build your list, you could skip this step and start promoting and driving traffic.

However, having a sales funnel in place will allow you to do the thing we all come to this game to do: make money. Sure, you can build your list and simply promote other people's products through affiliate marketing. And you should do that too. But having your own products and offers is extremely important.

The sales funnel has several parts to it which we will cover in more detail shortly. But an important point is; what I am suggesting here is optimal but not required. As mentioned, you can actually go ahead and start list building without this. But if you do, you're just leaving money on the table. So it is highly suggested to do each level. They are:

- **OTO (one time offer)**
- **Upsell #1**
- **Downsell #1**
- **Upsell #2**
- **Downsell #2**
- **Final Upsell**

In order to illustrate this and give you ideas on how to create your own sales funnel, I will illustrate the funnel me and my partner Eric Louviere just launched in this case study. Already mentioned before, it is called X2Fromula and you can see it live and in action by going to X2Formula.com.

The best way to go about this process is to lay everything out at once. Don't do one thing at a time. Read this entire process.

Ideally it is best to figure out what the offers are and then create them all. This will let you match things up and create a very congruent, easy to sell process.

What Is A Sales Funnel

A sales funnel is simply a process you will take your prospect through to get them to make one or more purchases from you. Usually, the best way is to have a low priced front end offer with higher priced back end offer(s).

The front end is what they see first. Since they've just gotten to know you, I recommend a lower price point with truly compelling copy.

The chances of someone purchasing higher ticket items go up as they get to know, like and trust you. That's not to say it is impossible to sell high ticket items (especially if you are endorsed by someone they already know, like and trust).

Our front end on the recent X2Formula.com offer is only $9. And it is converting nicely.

If they purchase that, they then see an OTO; short for One Time Offer. Now that they have given you their trust and their credit card, we offer them something at a higher price point.

Your funnel can lead in many directions having multiple upsells and downsells. The funnel we put in place has a first level upsell that is not too much more expensive than the first offer. They are given the choice to add this to their order or hit the no thanks button.

If they hit no thanks, they go to a downsell offer. This is a lower price than the first upsell for a product that is almost the same. It simply has certain features removed to make it more affordable.

If they take the first upsell, we offer them a second upsell. If they don't take the second upsell, they are given one more downsell.

There are no hard and fast rules here as to how you take them through the process and how many offers to show them. My opinion is the more the better. Maximizing the profit potential of each visitor is beneficial.

At the very least, you should have one offer to show them. Once they opt in, the next page they see should be the OTO sales page.

OTO – Your One Time Offer

This is the very first offering you will make. This should be a low priced product. I recommend somewhere between $1 and $14. We usually start at $7 to $9.

The benefit of this level is to cover your marketing expenses. So of all the steps in the sales funnel, this is one you really don't want to skip because it will cover your costs (or at least help cover them).

Your products should match your free giveaway product. It must be congruent. So if your free giveaway was on dieting, your OTO shouldn't' be on curing foot fungus.

Make your OTO a natural continuation of your free giveaway. This takes a little thought but it's not that hard. The customer is paying more money for more information. They are going to get more detail and process at each upward level.

Then you continue the conversation to the same target demographic. The new offer should match the previous offer.

This can be more of what they just got for free. If they got a traffic tactic as the free offer, the OTO may be 7 more of your hottest traffic tactics for just $9 or $11 or whatever the price you decide. It's not just free traffic with Youtube videos. It's also traffic with social media, Amazon, etc.

Another way to do this is to provide more detailed instructions in the paid version. So if the free report is the 'What' to do, the OTO can be the details on 'How' to do it step by step.

In the previous section I gave you an assignment to do. I told you to do the Content Curation method and come up with 5 things you can give away or sell. This is the time to review that list and pull together what you're going to use as your OTO, upsells and downsells.

The OTO Sales Page

In this process and at each of the next upsells and downsells, you also need to create the marketing. Each of your levels in the sales funnel will have a new sales page of its own.

This is going to be much easier to do than creating your squeeze page. The process of the squeeze page is always the hardest. Once you get past that, the rest is really much easier.

You've already done a ton of research and have created that first marketing message. As long as your upsells are congruent and continuations of what you have already done, much, if not all of what you will talk about on these sales pages are already there. You have to match what they got free and take it even further.

So when they get to this page, you will likely thank them for getting the free report. Let them know it's on the way to their inbox.

In X2Formula, our OTO page has a short headline, a video and a buy button. The buy button is set to delay so it does not appear until the moment that we share the offer price. This way, people have to listen to our sales message. Otherwise they're just going to click the buy button to see the price.

Step One: Watch This Very Quick Video!
(Do not click away from this page until
you've watched this video)

You Will Never See This Offer Anywhere
Else (EVER) And This Is Such A Special
Opportunity, You'd Be Insane To Miss It!

Add To Cart 🛒

VISA   DISCOVER   AMEX   PayPal

Our OTO is a PDF ebook. The free offer we have is a transcript from a coaching call that has a lot of what to do in it. The ebook really gets into the details of how to do things. For only $9 the ebook is tremendously underpriced.

When you create your sales page, remember, it's the copy that will sell it. You need to make an irresistible offer. So not only will they be interested in it, but they will completely forget about what the free offer even was. They're now really excited to get their hands on this new thing.

Upsell #1

If the OTO is going to pay for your traffic (coming later), your upsells will now make you a profit. You certainly don't need to do this to get started. Many people build big lists and then sell affiliate products and make big money with that method. However, I highly, HIGHLY recommend you create upsells.

A hungry market wants to buy products. And if you don't offer them the opportunities to purchase from you, someone else will. If you've done your homework and have found a red hot hungry niche they will demand opportunities to buy. And they will buy over and over again from you (if you offer the opportunity) and from many others in the same niche.

Another really important reason to offer upsells is branding. The more they buy from you, the more you become branded to them. And the more branded you are, the more money you will make in the long run.

This first upsell is the first offer they will see after they have become a customer. At this point, they have already given you their credit card to make a purchase from you. They have moved from prospect to customer.

The language we use is to thank them for getting the OTO and reward them by offering them this special limited opportunity.

Now the tech for this can be fairly complicated. We use 1Shopping Cart to handle our products and the entire upsell process. It can also be done programmatically. There are also many other fine products available to simplify the process.

Remember, the main idea here is to offer more advanced training or more advanced tactics as you work up through your sales funnel process. In X2Formula the first upsell is an affiliate training program that teaches affiliate techniques. We also offer a blueprint formula that was an ongoing training series that had been done and put into its own program.

Thank You!

Step 2! Now Watch This Quick Video!
(this video will be taken down and removed)

**I Want To Reward You For
Being A Mover And Shaker
Right Here And Right Now!**

VISA   DISCOVER   AMEX

No Thanks, I'm not interested in this once-only offer.

The page is very simple with only a headline and a video. This is the way we've chosen to do this and feel free to use the same method. But don't feel like you're limited to only this.

At the bottom of the page is the 'Add To Cart' button which is very prominent. We want to do everything we can to gently nudge our new customer to take action.

Below that button is a 'No Thanks' link. Much smaller and less impactful, this will take them away from this offer and onto the next step in the process which is the first downsell.

The price point for this can be anything you want. We try to make anywhere from $15 to $50 jumps.

Don't drive yourself crazy with pricing. When you get to the final steps, you will be able to perform tests to see what works and what does not.

You can do split tests where half the people see an offer at one price while the other half see it at a different price. Then you take the price that received the worse results and get rid of it.

Downsell #1

If they hit the 'No Thanks' link at the bottom of the first upsell page They will be taken to the first downsell. As we already discussed, (but this is worth really mentioning over and over again because it's super important), we want to invite them as much as possible to purchase from us. What better time to make as many offers as possible? After all, they have just purchased and this is the time when they are most likely to take action and purchase more.

The idea of the downsell is that we give them one more chance to say yes at a lower price. The person has decided to not purchase our upsell. It can be for a number of reasons. But the one we can control is the 'too expensive' reason. If that's the only reason they didn't buy, we can still get them to purchase from us here.

As you can see in the X2Formula sample below, we will address the financial concern. "Maybe the $35 was not a good enough deal for you. If so, we have one last chance for you to get this at only $17". We tell them, to be fair, we're going to remove something from the bundled package so lower the price.

Second Chance! WAIT!!

"if $35 is too much, how about an even better deal!?!"
(watch this 1 min video)

Ok, if $35 was not a good enough deal for you... how about $17 instead??

🛒 **Add To Cart**

VISA DISC VER AMEX

No Thanks, I'm not interested in this once-only offer.

What this process as a whole really allows us to do is to drive them through a sequence where they're getting things at different price levels and different program structures. It is unrealistic to think everyone will buy everything. Some will. But if we didn't have downsells, we would lose out on those who would not buy because of price. This will increase the amount of money we will make in total.

Upsell #2

At this point in the process they would have purchased the one time offer as well as upsell number one. They are now presented with a second upsell.

For this level, we offer a more valuable membership program. The cost for this one is higher and it gives them a lot more value. In our offer we are giving them the opportunity to get lifetime access to a membership site with live group coaching calls.

This has many more features to it than the previous programs thus allowing us to have a higher price tag. The beauty of information marketing is that you can create different programs on a regular basis and you will be able to reuse these programs and package them in different ways to create completely different offers.

In our program this is all we did. We took a cumulative bunch of other programs that we have done in the past and packaged them together. We also added the live and recorded group coaching which adds new content on a regular basis.

As we take someone through the process we are incrementing the price and value appropriately. So our first offer is for a PDF and is only $9. The first upsell is a $35 program. The second upsell makes another jump.

You can make your prices what ever you would like. However they should be logical jumps. So for example you would not make your OTO $9 and then make your first upsell $197. This would be too much of an increment and would not make much sense to your customer and they probably won't take the offer.

However, at $35 you need 7 people to buy to get around $197. There are always rule breakers here. It is possible that you can get enough people to buy at $197 to make it work.

Ultimately you do not know what will work and what won't work until you test it in action. We will talk more about this later. But if you desire to make it a $200 jump between your OTO and upsell, simply test it and see what works.

I prefer to make it a no-brainer. I like to keep the first bunch of offerings lower and increment them in smaller chunks. But eventually we take them to a higher ticket item. If you only have a high ticket item, go for it.

Downsell #2

At this point they have purchased the OTO, upsell number one and are now looking at upsell number two. If they choose the no thank you at upsell number two they will be directed to this process which is our final down sell offer.

This offer takes away part of the pricing and also takes away part of the product. The same way we did in downsell number one we are going to do here.

FINAL-FINAL step... Last Chance And Done!
(If $77 was too much for you, try this instead!!)

**Last Chance, Second
Chance Deal For List
Impact Club...**

🛒 **Add To Cart**

VISA DISC VER AMEX

No Thanks, I'm not interested in this once-only offer.

X2FORMULA

In downsell number one we offered them the same thing just with one thing missing at a lower price point. This is done to try to get the sale that we just missed but at a lower price.

Assuming they took upsell number one they have already spent $35 in our process. Next they're given a $77. In this downsell what we do here is remove the live coaching feature. So now they can purchase the exact same product minus the live calls at $35.

They will get the life time membership to all sorts of training however they will not be allowed to come onto live group coaching. This justifies asking for a lower price. This is the final downsell in our process. If they take this or not, the process ends here for us.

Final Upsell – High Ticket Offer

This is our big daddy program. This is our offer that they will see only if they have purchased every other upsell.

Understand that as your customer buys more in your sales funnel they're more likely to continue to purchase from you in the future. This is just another reason why offering a sales funnel with up and downsells are so important.

Some people will buy everything you have to offer. People like to buy period.

If you have picked a hungry niche there are customers out there that are going to buy whether you offer it or not. If you do not offer something, they will simply find somebody else who does offer it and purchase from them.

The final offer is usually the most expensive thing that you offer at this point. We offer our live one-on-one mentoring program. This is one-on-one private coaching.

Very high ticket price in the sales funnel. This is not for everyone, however some people will purchase it.

You can offer many different things. Coaching is a great thing to offer because it does command a high price point. You can offer high level training of any sort. You can offer a six week course. You can offer an ongoing high level membership program. There are no limits to what you can offer.

The only thing that you have to absolutely make sure of is that the value of your program at each level matches the price. When we price our products we always strive to over deliver whatever that content is. This way we always know were charging more than a fair price.

Step # 5 - Autoresponders

In this process, you will be getting your autoresponder system loaded with as much free content, teaching tips and offers as you can. This is simply the automatic sequence of events that will occur after the prospect enters their email address on your squeeze page.

We use Aweber as our autoresponder. There are a number of other systems available to you.

An autoresponder does exactly what the name suggests. It automatically replies to your contacts.

You will setup a sequence of emails to go out at intervals you specify. Our X2Formula sequence looks something like this:

Email Title	When It Goes Out
Welcome to the program	Immediately after they opt in
Teaching Tip #1	1 day after previous email
Our Offer #1	3 days after previous email
Teaching Video #1	3 days after previous email
Teaching Tip #2	4 days after previous email
Affiliate Offer #1	2 days after previous email

This is just a sample of our sequence. It is much longer than this and we add to it all the time. But this should give you the general flow.

It also follows a formula. That is the 'Give – Take' method. This means we send something out like a free tip. This doesn't cost anything. It is simply there to offer free advice and ideally build a relationship where our list gets to know, like and trust us.

After we offer a free tip, the next email would be to 'Take', or sell something. A lot of people make the mistake of thinking they have to just give, give, give and give. Then make apologies for trying to sell something.

The opposite is true. Giving nothing but free to your list is going to do something you may not intend. And that is to train them to expect to never pay for anything from you.

If your niche is a red hot and hungry one like we told you to find, they want very much to buy things. If you don't offer it, they will buy from someone who does. (Do I sound like a broken record yet?) And even worse, because they really do want to buy, they may actually stop opening your emails.

People may tell you straight out to stop sending them offers. They may say they don't want to buy anything.

What they are really saying is stop selling me stuff. People don't like being sold. But they love to buy. And you must present them with offers to buy.

Types Of Emails

There are essentially three different types of emails you will want to send:

1. Free tips designed to build good will
2. Offer emails
3. Transition emails that have a combination of both free tip and offer

The first two we already mentioned. The transition email is where you start with a free tip and transition into an offer. On the other hand, the offer email goes straight into the offer.

An example of a transition email is where you may be selling a traffic tactic formula. So you start by giving a free tip on traffic. At some point in the email you transition into your offer.

When you send an offer, there are two types you're going to promote:

- Yours
- Someone else's

99.9% of marketers will have an affiliate program. And when you promote their offer, you receive a commission.

You cannot create enough products of your own to satisfy the appetite of a hot niche. This is why you will want to promote other people's products as an affiliate.

Not to mention, the whole point of building a list is to make money. I don't care who tells you they are doing it for love of their people, or they say they just want to give back and they hate when people pitch. Yeah, yeah, yeah… whatever. They are in it to make money.

You do want to create enough of your own products and pitch enough of your stuff to keep your list interested in you. You need to build your brand before anyone else's.

When you do pitch other people's products, send a few free tips afterwards to keep them focused on you. Yes, you want them to buy but you also want them to stay engaged with your brand.

And just the way you would do with your own products, sell integrity first. Vet any product you plan to sell as an affiliate to make certain it delivers on it's promises.

Delivery Method

You can deliver your free content in a lot of different ways. I like to keep my list guessing. So I change things up. This keeps them opening those emails.

Many times the free content is simply within the email. Nowhere to click to. They just read the content right there.

I occasionally like to write the content as a blog post. Then I email enough of the content to wet their appetite with a read more link going to my blog.

The blog is sometimes written and sometimes video. I like to mix things up here too.

I have also placed content; written, video or audio on a webpage. I setup a page just for that free content and then my email will send them there through a link.

There are no limits to how you can deliver your free content. But the one thing I do prefer is to control where they go.

So for example, I don't like to deliver content to Youtube or Facebook. People tend to then get lost in that world and within minutes can't remember you or how they even got to Youtube in the first place.

Free Content Creation Method

Creating your free tips is just like what we covered in step #3. However, here we keep it much simpler.

I follow a couple rules when I create content. They are, quite simply:

1. Stay focused
2. Write to Homer Simpson

It's always important to keep things focused but even more so in these emails. You want to make sure they get read. And rambling or going off on unnecessary tangents is a sure fire way to get people ignoring you quickly.

Content emails should be tightly focused on one topic. As far as length, they should be as long as they need to be and no longer. If your content is focused and tight on the topic, it will be interesting no matter how long or short.

The second point speaks to how to communicate. When I am teaching, I try to use Homer as the ideal person to write to.

Homer Simpson is the really stupid dad on the show 'The Simpson's. Here's a great Homer quote that sums it up:

"Operator! Give me the number for 911!"

Not to say that my audience is stupid. I don't mean that at all. But when creating content, especially when you know a lot about your topic, it becomes way too easy to speak over the beginners or even a normal person's heads.

If you do that, you're done for. They will stop opening your emails because they can't understand a word you say.

So try to make all your content so that even Homer Simpson can understand it. If you do that, people will never get confused by any of your content.

Where To Find Tips

My favorite method for finding tips is to simply do Google searches on very specific areas. Like 'how to search optimize a video'. I will review a bunch of content that I find and use that as a starting point to write my own content.

Ezine Articles is a wealth of searchable content just waiting for you to come and get it. If you search on your topic and read just a few articles, very quickly you will be able to come up with a bunch of free tips to give to your audience.

Youtube is also a great wealth of information. Think of all the gurus in your niche and look to see what they've done on Youtube.

Not to mention, if you're on other marketer's lists, (and you should be), within your niche, you probably already get tips delivered right to your inbox every day. I keep a folder and save every marketers free tip emails in there. When I need an idea, I scan through that. I have emails saved going back over 5 years.

There is so much content readily available for us out there. The hardest part is simply freeing your mind enough to realize it's all right there at your fingertips.

Once again, don't steal someone else's content. You need to make it your own.

But for example, if you wanted to create a tip on how to shorten a URL, there are only so many ways to do it. Just add your own personality and it becomes yours.

The personality is what makes your tip unique. It's what makes you stand out from the rest of the market. It brands you to your audience and separates you from everyone else.

Who Are You

One very interesting trend I've seen lately is marketers disguising their names. So instead of it being from you or me, the from name is something like 'Update Center'.

This technique is used to trick people into opening the email. But I see it as a really poor strategy if you want a real business.

If you're going to brand yourself, it needs to be from you. They need to get used to seeing your name. Or your company name.

Step #6 – Affiliate Program

When you get down to step #8 you will begin driving traffic. One of those methods that every marketer, (at least 99% of them), will use is an affiliate program.

This is quite simply; free money. There are a lot of people out there with lists. The bigger the niche, the more people with big old lists.

And there are a lot of folks who just don't like or want to create content. They drive traffic to build their lists and then pitch affiliate offers.

Notice our affiliate link is on every page. When someone visits our squeeze page with all the traffic we will be driving in step #8, many of them will sign up right there. Others, we will seek out by simply emailing them and inviting them to promote in exchange for us promoting for them.

Platform Setup

The first step is to get a program that handles affiliate programs. This is just one of those expenses you can't get around.

We use 1Shoppingcart to manage our affiliate program. There are many systems out there that handle this at many different price points.

If you don't want to have your own platform, you can use something like Clickbank. The refund rates are higher on Clickbank but the fees are lower. You don't need to send out checks or really track anything; Clickbank does it all for you. Plus people looking for programs to sell can find you very easily on Clickbank with their search tool.

Commission Structure

This is where you have to decide how much to pay your affiliates. The bottom line is the more lucrative you make it for them, the more affiliates you will attract.

Personally, I will offer 75% to 100% on the first offer. This is the lower priced point of entry. I know if I buy ads I am going to give that all away to pay the cost so I look at this the same way with affiliates.

Most of the upsell and downsells we have are all 50% or higher. Offering less than 50% is pretty uncommon for normal information products. However, on our high ticket, high level programs that involve a great deal of our own personal time and also have a much bigger dollar amount we offer lower than 50%.

Marketing Materials

You need two types of marketing here. You need to create marketing that attracts affiliates and marketing they can use when they promote your offers.

Just like trying to persuade someone to buy from you, this must also be done with affiliates. You need a signup page that invites them and tells them all about your program. This should mostly speak to their needs and desires.

Then you need what is called 'swipe content'. This will be, at the least, emails they can use. This will have their personal affiliate link in the email. You can get pretty fancy and offer all sorts of materials like banner images.

Our page is pretty simple but I have seen people go all out here. Their affiliate pages look like any sales page you might see.

Make Money - Become An Affiliate

Promote for X2Formula now and earn as much as $816.25 per sale. Our front end offer is priced to pop like popcorn and you get 75% commission on that. There are two upsells and two downsells. You get 60% commission on the first level and 50% commission on the top level. That's $66.25 on our very affordable front end and upsell funnel.

You also have the opportunity to get the big payoff on our VIP coaching program. This is a high level coaching program (all clients coached by Eric Louviere and Mike Brooks) at a one time payment or an affordable 6 pay option.

Step 1: Fill in the form below

Step 2: Complete affiliate center registration on page 2

Step 3: Login and grab swipe emails under 'X2Formula Free Offer'

As of the writing of this book, our program was only recently launched. This page will become much more persuasive and sophisticated.

Step #7 – Tighten The Screws

At this point, you're just about ready to go. If you have ever put together one of those fancy swing sets, the last instruction is to go back and tighten up all the screws. This is so the swing doesn't come loose and launch a child into space.

This is what you need to do now. You have to go back and go through everything in your process and make sure it's working.

Your list may be different than mine but here's my checklist I used when we created X2Forumla.

- Squeeze page copy done and edited
- Opt in box works and goes to the right page
- Upsells and Downsells all work and go to the right page (test this with a real credit card and your gateway in test mode so your card does not get charged. Order using every possible sequence and make sure you're sent to the right place and get the right product delivered.
- Privacy, terms, contact, income disclaimers on the bottom of the page (all should open in a new browser).

- All copy has been proofed by other people
- All autoresponders proofed by other people
- Any links in autoresponder emails work and go to the right place
- Affiliates system tested and working
- Affiliate signup form on your pages, tested and working
- Tracking is in place and working – We use Google Analytics

Step #8 – Drive Traffic

This really is the easy part. Most people think it's so hard. Why do they think that? Because they want free traffic. Unfortunately there is no such thing.

You pay for traffic one way or another. If you spend all your time writing SEO niche articles, well, you just spent your time. And time is money.

We have a strategy that works like crazy and won't cost you as much as you might think. The method: Solo ad buys

Solo Ads

A solo ad is where someone with a subscriber list promotes your offer to their list for a fee. In every niche you will find people who sell solo ads.

There are many places you can find solo ads for your niche. To start, Google "Your Niche" plus "Solo Ad" and have a look at what comes up.

This is our favorite method. And for the most part, this is the only method we use to drive traffic. We don't do PPC, SEO, article marketing, blogging, or any of the crazy schemes you see out there from time to time. We just buy solo ads.

Why is that the only method we use? Because there is a ton of traffic to be purchased through this fairly inexpensive method and it works.

We begin by purchasing a certain amount of clicks. A click is simply one person clicking from the solo ad email to your offer. So we are essentially buying a set amount of people to see our offer.

Many solo ad sellers, especially smaller ones, will usually guarantee a minimum amount of clicks. If you do not get that minimum, they will send again. Bigger more sophisticated sellers expect that if you do not get the clicks, something was wrong with your copy so they won't guarantee minimums.

We begin by purchasing small amounts of clicks, maybe 100 to 500, from sellers that guarantee clicks. From here, we can track what the percentage is from click to opt-in to understand our opt-in rate. If it is 40% or better, we know we are doing well.

Then of course we track our rates of purchase. So we will drive a small amount of traffic in this step and then move to the next step where we test and tweak our conversions.

We keep doing this until we have solid numbers. Once we know our ads pay for themselves or come close, we will spend on more traffic. Once we are making money on ad buys, we open the flood gates because now it is, at the very least, free traffic.

Step #9 - Conversions

You have driven traffic. Now it's time to test, measure and tweak to consistently and constantly increase your conversions. The more effort you put into getting the conversions down, the higher your conversions will be. So doing certain things here will help you dramatically in the long run.

As mentioned, we look for these conversions before going back and driving massive traffic:

1. Opt in rate 40% or more
2. OTO rate is 10% or more
3. Upsell 1 rate is 30% or more

If these metrics are all at these points we know we will make money. Your offer may be different so you need to think through and create your own metric benchmarks.

The Infinite Loop Of Traffic And Conversions

These last two steps are tied together in and infinite loop. You will always come back here to test and tweak your marketing. The goal is to always and continually improve conversions.

Let's look at some math using our metrics from above:

We spend $250 to drive 500 clicks to our offer through a solo ad.

Using our metrics above, we get:

- At a 40% opt in conversion, 500 clicks will get us 200 opt ins
- At a 10% OTO conversion we will sell 20 units at $9 to bring us $180
- At a 30% Upsell 1 conversion we will sell 6 units at $35 to bring us $210
- This is a grand total of $390 we made $140 in profits.
- We may have made more with the other upsells and downsells but we are not yet measuring that

In this case, we know that we have profitable conversions. We may drive a few more solo ads to prove this out. After about 1,000 clicks, we will be pretty confident in the accuracy of our conversions.

If we do not need to tweak this, at this point we will open it to wider solo ads. We will now start to apply metrics to each level of upsell and downsell.

Then we simply tweak our offerings and copy to improve those conversions. And at some point when we are really confident, we will start to spend several thousand dollars to drive thousands of clicks.

As long as we're confident with our conversions, it doesn't matter how much money we spend, we will always profit. So really, the paid ads cost zero.

Conclusion

This is the best part of internet marketing. When you have gotten to this point, you are now a true internet marketer and have a real business that can make you money on autopilot.

All that hard work you did up front now is paying dividends. And now all you need to do is manage your affiliates, tweak your conversions and drive traffic.

That's it. You're in the game!

Bonus traffic tactic -
1,2,3,4, done

This technique will get you traffic. It will be free traffic and it will be the best kind; buyers. Here's what you need:

1: Salespage
2: private squeeze page
3: Nice ebook
4: Be willing to email 100 affiliates

What you do is setup a sales page offering whatever it is you're giving away for free. But here you put a price on it. This should be a real live working sales page with a buy button that if someone were to use it they will end up getting their credit card charged.

Next, you setup your private squeeze page. This is the back door where you give this product away for free.

Next, you send an email to 100 affiliates in your niche. Something like this:

Hi, my name is Mike Brooks. I have a product that sells for $47. Tell you what, I am trying to get my name out there so how about you offer this to your buyers as a free bonus. They get this on your behalf. They'll love you for it.

This may not work in the internet marketing market. They're pretty savvy. But the other niches are not.

Many will say no. Some will say yes. And all you need is a few.

If they say yes, simply give them the squeeze page to hook into their buyer thank you page. You can even have custom graphics made that they can then use on their buyer thank you page.

FREE

$357 Worth Of Internet Marketing Gold For You

To get even more money making secrets and to join our community, go to
www.internetmarketersguidebook.com
Just enter your email address and we will send you a wealth of free information.

About The Authors

Mike Brooks

Mike has been an entrepreneur since 2002. He quit his job to become an owner of a martial arts school. He took the school from a small hobby center to a half a million dollar a year operation.

In 2010 he sold the school to his partner and started an internet marketing company to help local businesses online. Mike had also been selling his own information products online for several years and eventually hired Eric Louviere as his mentor. They soon became business partners.

Eric Louviere

Eric has been in the Internet Marketing world since 2004 and became a full time online marketer in June of 2006. Eric's background is in offline marketing, advertising and sales.

In December of 2005, Eric made a commitment to push hard to replace his 90k per year corporate job with a full time income online from home. Six months later, Eric quit that 90k job as an advertising sales manager, packed his bags and moved from Houston to the hill country outside of Austin, TX (a place him and his wife always wanted to live).

www.ingramcontent.com/pod-product-compliance
Lightning Source LLC
Chambersburg PA
CBHW060639210326
41520CB00010B/1663